t

he
good
times
roll

an
incredible
cookbook

by nun
other than
sister
karol
jackowski

Ave Maria Press

Notre Dame, Indiana 46556

This book is printed and written with humble
and hearty thank-you's to the very best of
families, to friends forever near and far, to the
community of Saint Mary's College, to the Religious
community of Holy Cross and to the God who
lets the good times Roll in ordinary everyday
Routine.

Acknowledgements:
"On Sleep" © 1943 by Pantheon Books, Inc. Reprinted
from GOD SPEAKS, 2nd edition, by Charles Peguy,
translated by Julian Green, by permission of
Pantheon Books, a division of Random House, Inc.

"I Believe" used with permission of the
Cerabona family.

Recipes contributed by Henry and Shirley Jackowski,
Jackie Nutini, Debra and Mary Seremet, Kathleen
and Regina Rice, Mary Laverty, Barbara Saunders,
Estelle Nowosinski, Angie Cisnernos, Joan Holland,
Vicki Bernath, Mary Jane Silvia and Mary Anne
O'Donnell.

Cover Design: An abstract of nuns letting
_____ the good times Roll.

TABLE OF CONTENTS

THIS
RATHER
AMAZING
BOOK
is
DEDICATED
to
YOU.

A BLESSING IN THE BEGINNING

May the Blessing of Light be with you —
    Light outside and Light within.
May Sunlight ☼ shine upon you and warm your ♡
    'til it grows like a great peat fire
    So that the stranger may come
    and warm himself by it.
May a Blessed Light shine out of your two eyes
    like a candle set in two windows
    of a house, bidding the wanderer
    to come in out of the storm.
May you ever give a kindly greeting
    to those whom you pass as you go
    along the roads.
May the blessing of Rain - the sweet, soft Rain -
    fall upon you so that little flowers
    may spring up to shed their sweetness in the air.
May the Blessings of the earth - the good
    rich earth - be with you.
May the earth be soft under you when you
    rest upon it, tired at the end of day.
May earth rest easy over you when at last
    you lie under it.
May earth rest so lightly over you
    that your spirit may be out from under it
    quickly, and up, and off,
    and on its way to God.
                      —an old Irish Blessing

1.

★ DiPS ★

(for those on a diet who cheat)

Quickie

    1 pint sour cream
    1 package Good Season's Italian Dressing
      Mix

Mix together. Let it sit (stand or boogie)
in the fridge for 4 hrs. before serving.
if you don't have 4 hrs. it's good anyway.
Good with fresh veggies, chips, your little
finger or one-day-old pizza crusts.

The exotic Pre-formal Standard

    2 8oz. pks. cream cheese
    6 oz. ketchup
    2 tsp. Horse Radish
    1 tsp. lemon juice
    1 or 2 cans shrimp (or if you're in
       the bucks fresh shrimp.)

Mix well. Serve. Watch guests
fight over shrimp.

skip to the next dip →

*Our Lady of Guadalupe Dip

(for a little Arriba Arriba North of the Border)

1 2 LB. Box Velveeta cheese
2 8oz. cans Mexican tomatoes with Green Chilis.

Melt cheese in double Boiler →
Add tomatoes and chilis. Mix. Let sit (samba or siesta) for an hour or so to thicken. Serve with strong crackers or taco chips. ¡Ay caramba!

••• CURRY DIP •••
(if you need a dip in a curry... tee hee hee.)

1 cup sour cream
1 tablespoon (that's the big one) chili sauce
1 teaspoon (the middle one) dry mustard
1 teaspoon Worcestershire sauce
1 teaspoon curry powder
salt and pepper to taste.

Mix well and chill for 1 hour to mellow (have you ever been mellow...). Can also be made with yogurt for weight watchers.

---

*contributes to the Catholic character of this cookbook.

• GUACAMOLE GREEN •

2 ripe Avocados
1 onion
1 tomato
2 jalapeño peppers (fresh if possible)

Dice everything. Throw into Blender. Mix.
Then Liquify. Looks Gross but the
taste es terrífico.

★ POPEYE SPECIAL ★

1 package frozen spinach (chopped)
1 package Hidden Valley Ranch Dressing Mix
½ small chopped onion

Thaw spinach. Mix everything together.
Good with vegetables, crackers,
chips of all species and Rye-Crisps.

→ BACON-HORSERADISH DIPAROO ←

1 8oz. pk. cream cheese
3 tbls. sour cream
2 tbls. horseradish
6 tbls. crisp chopped bacon
             Mix. eat. yum.

The
only thing
We Have
to fear
is
fat
itself.
—Frank
Roosevelt

5.

PUNCHES

with and without the pows.

★ Pre-Christmas Christmas Party ★ 🎄 PUNCH 🎄

4 cans Hawaiian Punch
2 qts. Orange juice
4 lrg. Bottles 7-up
1 sm. Bottle tonic water

Mix. Add BUBBLY stuff last. (Always add BUBBLY stuff last.) Float scoops of sherbet on top. Maybe some orange slices too for eye appeal. Ice cubes. For pizzazz (and 21 yr. olds) add vodka or pink champagne. Serves 15-20.

WAHOO PUNCH

5 cups Southern Comfort (wahoo)
5 qts. 7-up
12 oz. fresh lemon juice
2 6 oz. cans frozen orange juice
4 6 oz. cans frozen lemonade

Chill ingredients. Mix. Add 7-up last. Add ice, orange and lemon slices. Invite 20 people and wahoo the night away.

6.

HOT BUTTERED RUM

1 LB. Butter
1 LB. BROWN SUGAR
1 LB. powdered SUGAR
1 Qt. vanilla ice cream
2 tsp. nutmeg
2 tsp. cinnamon

Blend well. Freeze. Keep in Freezer. Then take frozen mix out of freezer. Get a cup. Put two teaspoons of the frozen mix in a cup... . Add 1 jigger of rum. Pour in boiling water to fill cup. Stir. enjoy. calories: 1,000,000,000 per cup. But well worth it. You may even find yourself sneaking to the freezer and nibbling at the mix.

● a fascinating fact ●

Mozart wrote the music to "twinkle twinkle little star" when he was 5 years old.

NUN PUNCH (NUNS ARE FUN)

2 c. Southern Comfort (love that Southern Comfort)
2 c. Cranberry juice
6 oz. Lemon juice
24 oz. 7-up
 Mix. Float Lemon and orange slices.
         Serves 2-4.

MAKE UP YOUR OWN PUNCH

lemonade   Pineapple juice
Hawaiian punch   orange juice
7-up

Mix any or all of the above.
Float fruit or sherbet on top. You
can't go wrong.
              - OR -
Cranberry juice
Apple cider
7-up
              - OR -
      (fill in the blanks with your own mix)

1.
2.
3.
4.
5.
8.

NOG WITH EGGS

12 EGGS (BEAT till the color is LIGHT yellow)
MIX in SLOWLY with BEATER:
  1 LB. powdered SUGAR
  ¼ c. vanilla
  ½ tsp. salt
  2 cups RUM (if you wish) Let sit.
THEN: 2 qts. WHIPPING CREAM
      2 MORE cups RUM (if you wish)

Add last 2 ingredients after
MIXTURE sits for an HOUR OR SO.
THEN BEAT in together and MIX
well. Cover it and Let it do it's
thing in the fridge overnight.
 Before you serve, MIX well and
 SPRINKLE with nutmeg.

MOMENTS TO LIVE BY
Wine is Life to you if taken
    in Moderation.
Does SHE really Live who Lacks the
    wine which was created for her joy?
Joy of ♡, Good cheer and merriment
   are wine drunk freely at the
     proper time. SIRACH 31:27   9.

★ WASSAIL ★
(TERRIFFIC WITH FIGGY PUDDING)

1 Gallon Apple Cider
2 tsp. Whole Cloves
2 tsp. Whole Allspice
2 3" sticks of cinnamon
$2/3$ c. Sugar
2 Oranges with Cloves stuck
    in them →

Heat cider, cloves, allspice,
cinnamon and Sugar to Boiling,
Reduce Heat. Cover and simmer
about 20 min. Strain and pour
into punch bowl. (Make sure punch
bowl will Hold Hot stuff.) Float
oranges on top. Serves 10.

10.

"all things in moderation including moderation".

i think God said that.

11.

HOW TO BE ✱ A MOST SCINTILLATING HOSTESS AND/OR HOST...

Hints if you're going to serve alcohol:

1. **GIVE MORE THAN A DRINK:**
   introduce people who don't know each other. Get a conversation started... talk about Sister Karol... talk about this cookbook... Give someone a compliment whether they deserve it or not... Give them a laugh. You have more to give than just drinks.

2. **KEEP 'EM NIBBLING:**
   Not just later on, but while your guests are drinking. That's important. It slows down the rate at which people drink.

3. Offer soft drinks.

One third of the adult population chooses not to drink at all. And many who do sometimes prefer not to. So offer a choice.

4. Dinnah is served.

If you're serving dinner or a snack do it before it's too late. If the cocktails go on for hours, the guests won't know what they had for dinner.

5. IF... someone drinks too much at your party, you are responsible. That's what it means to be a very scintillating hostess or host. See that the drinkers get home safely. But don't let them drive.

6. Have a blast.

A veritable blast.

14.

·.··COOKIES COOKIES·.··

Supernatural Brownie Cookies

½ c. Butter
4 sq. semi-sweet chocolate
2 c. sugar
2 tsp. vanilla
2 c. flour

4 eggs
2 tsp. Baking powder
¼ tsp. salt
½ c. nuts

Melt chocolate and butter. Add sugar and vanilla and mix well. Add eggs one at a time. Sift in dry ingredients. Add nuts and mix well. Cover and chill in fridge 2-3 hrs. or overnight. Form into small balls (ooooooo) — roll in powdered sugar. Bake on greased cookie sheet at 350° for 12 min. People kill for these.

MOMENTS TO LIVE BY

"I have food to eat of which
You do not know."

- Jesus

15.

PEANUT BLOSSOMS

1 ¾ c. flour
1 tsp. baking soda
½ tsp. salt
½ c. sugar
½ c. brown sugar

½ c. margarine
½ c. peanut butter
1 egg + 1 egg = 2 ◯◯
2 tbls. milk
1 tsp. vanilla

and 48 kisses

MWAH!

SMACKITY SMACK!

KISSY KISSY.

KISSY!

Combine all ingredients except ⬯'s (kisses). Mix on lowest speeds until dough forms. Shape dough into balls. Roll in sugar → ◉ ◉ ◉ ◉. Place onto greased cookie sheet. Bake 10-12 min. at 375.° Top each with a kiss immediately. (kiss each). Press down so cookies crack around edges → ⬯.

★ CHOCOLATE CHIP COOKIES ★
Use Toll House recipe on the back of the chocolate chip bag. it's the best.

CONGO SQUARES

(from the Congo)

2¾ c. flour
2½ tsp. baking powder
½ tsp. salt
⅔ c. shortening
3 eggs
½ c. chopped nuts
1 big bag chocolate chips
2¼ c. brown sugar

Melt shortening, add brown sugar. Cool slightly. Add eggs, one at a time. Beat well after each. Add dry ingredients, nuts and chocolate chips. Bake in 9 x 11 pan at 350° for 25-30 min.

When cool cut into squares.

P. B. C.'s (peanut butter cookies)

Preheat oven to 375°

Beat until soft:
   ½ c. butter or shortening

Add gradually and blend:
   ½ c. firmly packed brown sugar
   ½ c. granulated sugar

Beat in:
   1 egg
   1 c. peanut butter
   ½ tsp. salt
   ½ tsp. baking soda
   ½ tsp. vanilla

Sift and add:
   1-1½ c. all purpose flour

Roll dough into small balls →

Place them on a greased cookie sheet →

Press flat with a fork →

Bake 10-12 minutes.

Makes about 60 1½" cookies.

enough for 2-3 students.

18.

Gingerbread Persons

Preheat oven to 350°:
Blend: ½ c. Butter
         ½ c. White or Brown Sugar

Beat in: ½ c. dark Molasses
Sift: 3½ c. all purpose flour
Resift with: 1 tsp. Baking Soda
             ¼ tsp. Cloves
             ½ tsp. Cinnamon
             1 tsp. Ginger
             ½ tsp. salt

Add sifted ingredients to Butter mixture alternately with ¼ c. water. May have to work dough with your hands if the mixer poops out. Roll any thickness you like. Bake about 8 min. or longer according to thickness. Test for doneness by pressing cookie's belly with your finger. If it springs back, they're ready.

ice with ¼ c. powdered sugar and a few drops of water — drop or two of coloring if you want to dress them in the latest threads.

19.

SNICKER DOODLES

Mix Well: 1 c. soft shortening
1½ c. sugar
2 eggs

Sift and stir in: 2¾ c. flour
2 tsp. cream of tartar
1 tsp. baking soda
¼ tsp. salt

Chill dough. Roll into small Balls ooooooooooooooooo. Roll them in a mixture of two tbls. sugar and 2 tsp. of cinnamon. Bake 8-10 minutes at 400°.

People will never snicker at these fine doodles. no sireee bob.

20.

Potato chip cookies

½ LB. MARGARINE

½ LB. BUTTER

1 C. SUGAR

2 EGGS

(MIX ALL OF THAT TOGETHER)

1½ tsp. vanilla

3½ C. FLOUR

2 C. CRUSHED potato CHIPS

Mix well and drop on ungreased cookie sheets. Bake for 12-15 minutes at 350°. Makes about 75 cookies.

Don't say "OH ick, potato CHIP cookies. HOW GROSS."
These are some terrific cookies.

Gingersnaps

¾ c. Butter
2 c. sugar
2 eggs
2 tsp. vinegar
½ c. dark molasses

Mix ALL of that well. Add:
3 tsp. ginger
¼ tsp. cloves
1 tsp. cinnamon
3 ¾ c. flour
1 ½ tsp. Baking soda

Blend it all together. Form dough into small Balls ooooooooooooooooo.
375° Bake for 10-15 min. on greased cookie sheet. For a real treat put a half of a marshmallow (cut side down) on semi-Baked cookies. Put them back in and let them bake 5 more minutes.

22.

OLD FASHIONED BUTTER COOKIES

1 c. *butter and sugar
2½ c. flour
2 tbsp. orange juice
   (yes, orange juice)

1 egg
1 tsp. baking powder
1½ tsp. vanilla

Cream butter, sugar and egg until light and fluffy. Beat in flour, baking powder, orange juice and vanilla until smooth. Chill 2-3 hrs. Should be firm enough to be rolled. Preheat oven to 400.° Roll on well floured surface to ⅛-¼". Cut out. Place on ungreased cookie sheet. Bake 6-10 min. or until golden brown on edges. Cool. Frost.

BUTTER CREAM FROSTING

Blend: 3 c. powdered sugar
        ⅓ c. soft butter
Add: 1-2 tbsp. milk
      1 tsp. vanilla
Beat till fluffy.

* sneaky secret: use margarine with 1 tsp.
     butter flavor per stick of margarine

OATMEAL COOKIES

In 1978 a group of 11 college students inhaled 173 of these.

1 c. Raisins
¾ c. Margarine
1½ c. sugar
2 eggs
1 tsp. vanilla
2 c. flour

1 tsp. baking soda
1 tsp. salt
1 tsp. cinnamon
½ tsp. baking powder
½ tsp. cloves
2 c. oatmeal
1 c. chopped nuts

Heat oven to 400°. Mix margarine, sugar, eggs and vanilla. Blend in remaining ingredients. Drop by spoonfuls on ungreased cookie sheet. Bake 10-12 minutes.

HAPPY BIRTHDAY
DEAR
YOU.

At least 10 million people are having a birthday today.

★.★ Pineapple Cookies ★.★
(if you hate pineapple move on)

1 c. shortening
1 c. brown sugar
1 c. white sugar
1 c. crushed pineapple
1 c. nuts
1 tsp. vanilla

2 eggs
4 c. flour
½ tsp. salt
½ tsp. soda
2 tsp. baking powder

Combine everything and beat till well mixed. Drop by teaspoons onto a lightly greased cookie sheet. Bake at 350° until lightly browned (about 10 min.). Remove and cool 5 min. before taking from the pan.

● Cheese Bars ●

Mix and press into a 9x13 pan:
   1¼ c. crushed graham crackers
   1 c. flour
   1 c. chopped nuts
   ½ c. sugar
   ¾ c. melted margarine

Bake 12 min. at 350°. Do not overbake.

more. →

25.

FILLING: 2 8 oz. pkg. cream cheese
$\frac{2}{3}$ c. sugar
2 eggs
2 tbls. lemon juice
1 tbls. milk

Blend ingredients together, pour into crust. Bake at 350° for 20-25 min. <u>Double</u> the filling for a deeper bar.

BANANA OATMEAL BARS

$1\frac{1}{2}$ c. flour
1 c. sugar
1 tsp. baking soda
1 tsp. salt
$\frac{1}{4}$ tsp. nutmeg
$\frac{3}{4}$ tsp. cinnamon
$\frac{3}{4}$ c. shortening

1 egg, well beaten
1 c. mashed banana
$1\frac{3}{4}$ c. oatmeal
1 c. chopped nuts
1 pkg. chocolate chips

Sift first six ingredients together. Cut in shortening. Add egg, banana, oats and nuts. Beat well. Add chocolate chips. Spread into greased 9x13 pan. Bake at 350° for 25 min.

THE NEXT SECTION
   OF THIS SCINTILLATING
COOKBOOK INCLUDES YOUR
   FAVORITE

- ☒ PIES
- ☒ CAKES
- ☒ CUPCAKES
- ☒ MUFFINS
- ☒ BREADS
- ☒ OTHER
     FOOD
     STUFFS

MADAME LAZONGA'S CHEESE PIE

(the one that made her famous and loved)

GRAHAM CRACKER CRUST

    1¼ c. graham cracker crumbs
    ¼ c. sugar
    6 tbls. butter (or margarine)

Mix crumbs, sugar and butter. Press into 9" pie plate. Place in freezer 15 min. or chill in fridge 1 hour or buy the ready-made ones.

EUPHORIC FILLING

    2 8 oz. pkg. cream cheese
    ½ c. milk   ¼ c. sugar
    1 tbls. vanilla
    1 can cherry or blueberry
        pie filling (or crushed pineapple)
    2 envelopes Dream Whip Mix

In a large bowl mix everything (except pie filling). Beat until smooth and creamy. Pour into crust. Chill 4 hrs. Spread with pie filling.

PeRSONaL COMMents and MeMORIeS ReGaRding the LazONGa cHeesecake:

1. OH MY God.
2. M-M-M-MWaH.
3. A-A-A-A-H.
4. MORe. MORe. MORe.
5. (OTHER) _____

PUMPKIN PIE

FILLING:

- 3 eggs →ooo
- 1 can (1LB) pumpkin
- 3/4 c. Brown sugar, firmly packed
- 1 tsp. cinnamon
- 1/8 tsp. allspice
- 1/8 tsp. ground cloves
- 1/2 tsp. ground ginger
- 1 c. pet evaporated milk

Beat eggs until foamy. Add pumpkin, Brown sugar, cinnamon, all spice, cloves, ginger and milk. Beat until thoroughly mixed. Pour into prepared shell. Bake at 350° for 40 min.

HOW to make a pie shell? fear not... ⟶

*Steps for making a pie shell:

1. Buy Pie Crust sticks...

2. Buy frozen pie shells...
                    OR
            MESS WITH THIS:

    1 LB. SHORTENING
    5 c. flour (not sifted)
    1 TBLS. SUGAR
    1 TBLS. SALT

a. Cut shortening into other ingredients.

b. In a measuring cup beat 1 egg and add enough water to make 1 cup of liquid.

c. Pour liquid into flour mixture and mix well. Set for 10 minutes. Divide into seven balls and roll them in flour. Makes enough for 7 crusts. May be wrapped in foil and frozen. A good deal.

* This cookbook thinks of everything doesn't it?

A STORY

i REMEMBER FROM WHEN i WAS a VERY MUCH YOUNGER TURTLE, THAT i HAD a friend WHO WAS not quite LiKE THE REST of US. HE WAS always WANDERING off BY HImself WHEN HE GREW tired of the Games we never ceased to enjoy.

One day HE BuiLt a flying MACHine. WE WERE all very excited aBout His fLying MACHine, foR no turtLE HAD ever LEFT tHE GROUND Before. MY friend, LAUGHING at OUR FEARS, CLImBed Into His flying MACHine, and spun off into tHE SKY, WAVING at US from a GREAT HEIGHt. WHEN HE RETURNED to tHE GROUND He spoke to us of strange siGHts in BReatHLEss WORds WHicH we COULd not understand.

EacH day HE Boarded His flying MACHine and soaRed off into tHE clouds; eacH day His words GREw moRE difficult to comprehend. FeaRING tHat He was just a LittLE Mad, we decided to iGnoRE Him and continue in OUR Games. FinalLY one day he disappeaRed in a Bank of clouds and was never seen aGain.

$$\Large \searrow \searrow \to$$

From time to time i HeaR RuMoRs from travelling stranGeRs aBout My friend. Some say He cRasHed into a lake and went straiGHt to tHe BottoM. OtHeRs contend that He GRew amBitious and flew directLy into tHe sun. But someHow i feel He is stiLL up tHeRe in His flying MacHine, seeinG siGHts that no turtle Has ever seen.

-autHoR unknown

✳ miniature cheese cakes ✳

3   8 oz. pks. cream cheese
1   c. sugar
5   eggs
1½ tsp. vanilla

Cream above ingredients and pour into cupcake papers at 350° for 30-40 min. Remove and cool 5 min. (use foil cupcake papers).

Place in the center of each a picture of Sister Karol... or a spoonful of: 1 c. sour cream
                        ½ tsp. vanilla
                        ½ c. sugar

Then put a maraschino cherry on top and bake for 5 min. at 300°

Know what?

Deer have no gall bladders.

THE MOST WANTED SOUR CREAM COFFEE CAKE IN THE WORLD

1 c. Butter (or margarine)
2 c. sugar
2 eggs
1 c. sour cream

2 c. sifted flour
1 tsp. baking powder
¼ tsp. salt
1½ tsp. vanilla

topping: ½ c. chopped nuts
¼ c. brown sugar
1½ tsp. cinnamon

Beat butter with sugar. Add eggs, sour cream and vanilla and continue beating. (By this time you'll be pretty beat...get it?) Add flour, baking powder and salt. Make topping by combining nuts, brown sugar and cinnamon.

Grease (is the word...) and flour a Bundt pan. Put ⅓ batter in bottom of pan. Sprinkle ½ of topping on top. Add more batter and the rest of the topping. Add last of batter. Bake at 350° for 50-60 min. Cool 15 min. then turn onto plate.

♡ Red Velvet Cake ♡

2 c. sugar
½ c. butter
3 eggs
1 tbls. vinegar
1 tbls. cocoa
2 oz. Red food
     color

2½ c. flour
½ tsp. salt
1½ tsp. baking soda
¼ tsp. baking powder
1 c. buttermilk
1 tsp. vanilla

Cream sugar and butter; add eggs. Make a paste of vinegar, cocoa and food coloring; add to creamed mixture. Add dry ingredients to mixture alternately with buttermilk. Add vanilla and blend thoroughly. Bake in 3 cake pans at 350° for 30 min.

♡ ICING ♡

1 c. milk
3 tbls. flour
1 c. sugar
1 c. butter

1 c. chopped pecans
OR
1½ c. coconut
1 tsp. vanilla

Cook milk and flour until thickened. Set aside to cool. Cream sugar and butter; add to cooled flour mixture. Add remaining ingredients, mixing well.

Roseannadanna

BANANA BREAD ↓ ↓ ↓

¼ c. shortening	1½ c. flour
1 c. sugar	1 tsp. salt
1 egg	1 tsp. soda
3 ripe bananas	½ chopped nuts

Mix shortening, egg and sugar well. Add bananas (mashed), flour and mix well. Add soda. Nuts optional but add last if using them! Bake in well greased and floured loaf pan at 350° for 1 hour.

Tasty.

CARROT CAKE

1½ c. oil
2 c. sugar
4 eggs
3 c. grated carrots
½ tsp. salt
3 c. flour

½ c. walnuts
2 tsp. baking soda
2 tsp. baking powder
2 tsp cinnamon
1 tbls. cocoa

Mix dry stuff. Pour in oil. Add eggs.
Stir in carrots and nuts. Mix well.
Bake 1 hr. at 350°

Cream Cheese frosting

¾ c. powdered sugar (sifted)
Mix until soft and fluffy:
    3 oz. cream cheese
    1½ tbls. cream or milk
Beat in sugar. Add 1 tsp. vanilla
and ½ tsp. cinnamon.

  Best spread on warm cakes.
  Good to let it stand over
   boiling water for 10-15 min.
   to get the raw taste of the
   sugar out.

Apple Nut Cake

1 c. oil
2 c. sugar
2 eggs
2 tsp. vanilla
1 tsp. cinnamon

Mix and add:
2 c. flour
½ tsp. salt
1 tsp. soda
3 c. chopped apples
1 c. walnuts

Put in greased tube pan.
Bake at 350° for
50-55 minutes.

A FAVORITE FACT:

In the Eskimo Bible, Jesus
is not referred to as the
"Lamb of God"
But as "God's seal-pup."

☆ Piña Colada Cake ☆

CAKE:

1 pk. (2 layer size) white cake mix
1 pk. (4 serving size) coconut cream
                          pudding mix
4 eggs $\frac{1}{3}$ c. dark rum
$\frac{1}{2}$ c. water   1 c. flaked coconut
$\frac{1}{4}$ c. oil

FROSTING:

1 can 8 oz. crushed pineapple (in juice)
1 pk. coconut cream pudding mix
$\frac{1}{3}$ c. rum
1 9oz. container frozen whipped
                    topping thawed

Mix cake ingredients (except coconut)
in large bowl. Beat about 4 min.
Pour into 2 greased + floured 9" pans.
Bake at 350° for 25-30 min. Cool.
Fill + frost. Sprinkle with coconut. Chill.
Refrigerate leftover cake.

For frosting, combine all ingredients
except whipped topping in bowl. Mix
till blended. Fold in whipped topping.

This cake is something else.

40.

Cream Cheese Fudge

2 3oz. pkgs. cream cheese
2 tbls. milk
4 c. powdered sugar
4 sq. unsweetened chocolate (melted)
1 tsp. vanilla
1 tsp. rum
dash of salt
1½ c. chopped walnuts

Beat cheese and milk till smooth...
Gradually beat in sugar and blend
in chocolate. Stir in rest of stuff.
Press lightly into greased 8" sq.
pan and cover top w/ ½ c. nuts.
Cut into squares after chilled
until firm.

FAT CITY.

○ M. JANE's DUTCH APPLE PIE ○

8 large tart apples, peeled and sliced
3/4 c. sugar
2 tsp. cinnamon
1/4 tsp. nutmeg
2 dashes salt
3/4 c. flour

Mix. Put into crust... actually makes
2 pies.

Sprinkle topping of:
3/4 c. flour
3/4 c. brown sugar
1/2 c. butter
add nuts if you like.

Bake 45 min. at 350°.
Cover top with foil for last 10 min.
So sugar and crust don't burn.
Serve with ice cream or cheddar
cheese.

Pineapple pound cake

½ c. Butter
½ c. Shortening
2¾ c. Sugar
6 eggs
3 c. Flour

1 tsp. Baking powder
1 tsp. Vanilla
¼ c. Milk
¾ c. Crushed pineapple
(drained)

Turn on some Hawaiian music.
Cream Butter, shortening and sugar.
Add eggs. Beat well. Add dry stuff.
Add milk, vanilla and pineapple. Mix
well. Bake at 325° for 1½ hrs.

Topping: ¼ c. Butter
1½ c. powdered sugar
1 c. crushed pineapple

Heat in saucepan.

Spoon on top of cake.

Dress up like a princess (or prince)
and serve.

NANNER CAKE

½ c. BUdder
1½ c. SHUGGeR
2 eGGz
2 c. flower
¼ tsp. B. powdR
¾ tsp. B. sewda
1 tsp. sault

¼ c. sower creem
3 nanners masHed
1 tsp. vanillaH

CReam Butter and sUGaR. Add eggs.

Add sifted dry ingRedients,
SOUR CReam, bananas and
vanilla.

Bake for 30 min. at 350°
in 2 GReased and floured
cake pans.

Cupcakes: 15-20 minutes.

AnotHeR RoseAnne RoseanneR danner
favorite.

44.

Diana Ross's Supreme Cake

1 Box yellow cake mix
4 eggs
1 Box instant vanilla pudding
1 c. sour cream
½ c. oil
½ c. cream sherry

Mix. Beat for 10 min. and
   pour into angel food pan.
Bake at 350° for 50-60 min.

Mix some powdered sugar
with sherry and drizzle

on top
for frosting.

HONEY WALNUT BREAD
(like the monks make)

1 c. milk
1 c. honey
1/4 c. soft butter
2 eggs beaten
2 1/2 c. whole wheat flour
1 tsp. salt
1 Tbls. baking powder
1/2 c. walnuts

Mix milk and honey over heat until blended. Beat in butter, eggs, flour, salt and baking powder until well mixed. Fold in nuts.

Put in ungreased loaf pan. Bake 1 hour at 325°; cool 15 min. in pan. Cool before slicing.

Divine.

HARVEY
WALLBANGER
CAKE

1 pk. Orange Supreme Cake Mix
1 pk. instant vanilla pudding mix
½ c. oil
¾ c. orange juice
4 eggs
¼ c. vodka
¼ c. Galliano

Mix. Put into greased and floured tube cake pan. Bake at 350° for 45-55 min. (This one's a real wallbanger.)

★ H. WALLBANGER FROSTING ★

1 c. sifted powdered sugar
1 tsp. orange juice
1 tbsp. Galliano
1 tsp. vodka

Pour on warm cake.

47.

A
PROVERB

The righteous
eats to satisfy
the need
But the wicked's
stomach
never has
enough.

PROVERBS
13:25

48.

A GOOD PIE

1 4oz. Box pistachio pudding Mix

1 9oz. thing of frozen Cool Whip (thawed)

1 10oz. can of crushed pineapple
  in it's own juice.

Mix all of those together

Put into a GRAMCRACKER (new spelling)
CRUST OR CRUSHED Chocolate
Cookie crust.

Sprinkle with Chocolate
Sprinkles.

Put in the fridge for
an HOUR OR two.

A LITTLE KNOWN FACT

A sneeze can travel as fast
as 100 Miles per HOUR.

BROWNIES

4 ☐☐ ☐☐ Unsweetened Chocolate
2/3 c. Shortening
2 c. Sugar
4 eggs ⟶ ○○○○
1 tsp. Vanilla
1¼ c. Flour
1 tsp. Baking powder
1 tsp. Salt
1 c. Chopped nuts

Heat oven to 350°. Grease 9"x13" pan. Melt Shortening and Chocolate over low Heat. Blend with Sugar, eggs and Vanilla. Mix in Rest of stuff. Spread in pan. Bake 30 min. or until Brownies pull away from pan. Cool. Cut. Makes Lots.

DUMP CAKE

1 can crushed pineapple
1 can cherry pie filling
1 pk. yellow cake mix

DUMP cherry pie filling in bottom of *baking dish. DUMP crushed pineapple on top of cherry pie filling. DUMP cake mix and crumble over top of mixture. Then melt 1 stick of margarine and slowly pour over top. OR cut little pats of margarine and scatter them on top. Bake at 375° for 45 min. Cool. Cut. Serve.

* i use an angel food pan or springform pan... which means you let it cool 5-10 min. then DUMP it on a plate, cut and serve.
   You won't believe how good this one is.

Dad's Pumpkin Pie

1 9" pie shell baked
1 1LB can pumpkin (not the mix...)
1 pumpkin can full of whole milk
2 c. sugar
1/4 tsp. salt

Mix all together in a pot (aluminum pot preferred) and bring to boil. When it comes to a full boil mix these ingredients well and add to pumpkin:

1/2 c. sugar	1/4 tsp. cloves
1/2 tsp. ginger	1 tsp. cinnamon
2 oz. cornstarch	4 large eggs ↓
1/4 c. water	OOOO

Blend well and stir continuously until thick. Take off heat and pour into aluminum or pyrex pans to cool - stir pumpkin mix every 10 min. or so to prevent skin forming on top - when cooled fill pie shells (already baked ones).

Put pies in fridge for 3-4 hrs. Serve.

These are no bake pies.

52.

~ I BELIEVE ~

I Believe in the wind for it whispers love.

I Believe in the stars for they shine
endlessly into the night.

I Believe in myself because I'm worth
believing in.

I Believe in life for from it all good
things come.

I Believe in truth, because nothing
is hidden.

I Believe in God because His creation
is my living proof.

I Believe in Jesus for I see Him
in other people.

I Believe in people because they are
basically good.

I Believe in love, for it makes things
right.

I Believe in death because it is a
new beginning.

But most of all I believe if faith and hope
are alive, then dreams can become realities
and life is worth living and there is no
end; just an endless corridor passing
into a quiet eternity.

Judy Cerabona
1957 - 1978

THE MAIN EVENTS

★ CHicKen cacciaToRe ★

1 CHicKen oR parts equivalent
(i Love to say tHat: "parts equivalent")

BRown in ButteR and SHeRRy.
Add 1 15oz. can seasoned tomatо
Sauce witH tomatо Bits.

1 can MUSHRooMS

1 pK. ItaLian DRessing Mix

(can also add GReen pepper, italian
Seasoning , GaRLic and Bay Leaf
to taste ...)

COOK one HOUR.

～～～ STROGANOFF FOR SIX ～～～

2 LBS. steak, cut into thin strips
          OR bite size CHUNKS.
Butter
1½ LBS. FRESH MUSHROOMS
   Seasoned salt and seasoned pepper
½ C. SHERRY
2 C. SOUR CREAM

In LARGE skillet sauté meat in BUTTER
until BROWN but still RARE and juicy,
about 3-4 MIN. REMOVE from pan and
set aside.

Add MORE BUTTER to pan and BRIEFLY
sauté MUSHROOMS. Add seasoned salt
and pepper to taste. Add SHERRY
and cook till BUBBLING →

Return meat to pan. OVER
VERY LOW HEAT stir in SOUR CREAM
THOROUGHLY. Heat well but
DON'T YOU DARE BOIL
          it.

B. S.
(Bean salad)

1 can string beans
1 can wax beans
1 can kidney beans
1 large onion
1 c. celery (cut up)
3/4 c. oil
3/4 c. sugar
1/4 c. vinegar
1 tsp. salt
1/2 tsp. pepper

Drain beans and mix.
Let sit overnight.
That's a lot of B.S.
(Bean salad)

ANGIE'S TACOS

(ANGIE WORKS WITH MY MOM AT THE PHONE COMPANY)

2 LBS. CUBED PORK OR TACO MEAT
Cook pork till BROWN (about 20 min.).
Add LARGE cooking spoon of flour...
Sprinkle over meat.
Get some dried red chili peppers...the
Hot ones. Put in a saucepan half
filled with water. Wash, stem and
seed about 7-10 chilis...simmer
till soft.

THen in a Blender put a 16 oz.
can of tomatoes. Add chilis,
some Garlic powder (about four
shakes), onion powder (about four
shakes). Mix well in Blender.

Pour sauce over meat. Add
water to desired thickness.
Simmer 20 min. Serve in
soft taco shell.

Dad's special Chops

4 PORK CHOPS
½ c. BREAD CRUMBS (unseasoned)
1 EGG
5 TBLS. Soy sauce
2 TBLS. dry SHERRY
   PINCH of GINGER (BUT do not pinch GINGER)
   PINCH of GARLIC powder

Scatter Bread Crumbs on a plate.
Beat rest of ingredients (except chops) in
a SHALLOW BOWL. Dip your chops first
in egg mixture, then in CRUMBS,
coating both sides.

   ARRANGE chops in a single file
on a SHALLOW non-stick BAKING
   pan. (FOR no-fat frying spray with
   those no-fat sprays).
Bake uncovered at 350° for
25-30 min. Turn and bake
20-25 min. LONGER.

YOUR CHOPS will love these CHOPS.

Spiffed Up Baked Beans

2 18oz. cans Pork and Beans
¾ c. Brown Sugar
1½ tsp. Mustard
½ c. catsup
1 tsp. vinegar

Uncooked Bacon

Mix. Put Bacon strips on top.
Bake 1½ HRs. at 325°.

The Mona Lisa Has no
eyeBrows.
(it was the fashion of Renaissance Florence
to shave them off)

★ MOM'S KAPUSTA ★
(POLISH SAUERKRAUT WITH SPARERIBS)

2 LBS. SPARERIBS
  Put them in a pot (BIG one). Cover them with water. Toss in a couple of Bay Leaves... a clove of GARLIC.
    Boil and simmer 1 HOUR.

2 QTS. SAUERKRAUT
  Wash KRAUT REAL Good to Get the sours out.
Drain some of the water out of the pot of RIBS... (most of it)... put KRAUT in with RIBS and remaining water. Add 1 chopped onion---
6 OR 7 pieces of dried MUSHROOMS.
    Let simmer all day. After 3-4 HOURS Add some crisp, chopped Bacon (5-6 slices) and 3 tbls. flour, some cut up potatoes and let simmer some more.
  You can also add Polish sausage.

German apple pancakes
••• that puff up •••

1 c. sifted flour
½ tsp. B. powder
 pinch of salt
1 c. milk
5 (yes 🖐️?) eggs
2 tbls. melted butter
thinly sliced apples sautéed in butter.

Mix and sift dry ingredients.
 Stir in milk. Add eggs one at a time,
 beating each separately in batter.
 Add melted butter.

 Pour into hot greased skillet.
 Put on direct heat for 1 minute,
 then bake in hot oven (425°)
 till brown, puffy and edges
 curl up (20-25 min).
  Before putting in oven put
 apples, sugar and cinnamon
   on top of pancake.
     Fat Fat City.

BBQ RIBS

(sauce Recipe peR pound of RiBBos)

2 tBLs. maRGaRine
1 med. onion cHopped
1 cLove GaRLic (minced)
½ c. catsup
2 tBLs. vineGaR
½ tsp. taBasco
1 tBLs. BRown suGaR
1 tsp. saLt
1 tsp. dRy mustaRd
¼ c. wateR.

BRinG aLL to a BoiL. Bake RiBs at 350°
foR 30 min. PouR sauce oveR RiBs and
Bake foR an HouR LonGeR.

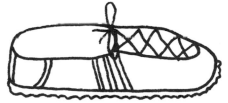

Americans spend moRe tHan
$125 BiLLion a yeaR on
sneakeRs.

★ ★ Pepper Steak ★ ★

1 LB. Beef tenderloin cut in 2" strips
2 Green peppers cut in thin strips
MUSHROOMS
1/4 c. OIL
1 tsp. OREGANO
1 clove GARLIC
1/4 tsp. pepper
1/4 c. SHERRY
2 tomatoes cut up
1 Beef Bouillon CUBE
(Getting tired?)
Garlic Salt (a few shakes)
1 small onion
2 tBLS. Soy Sauce
2 tBLS. water
1 tBLS. Cornstarch
1/2 tsp. Salt
1/2 tsp. SUGAR

Pound Steak (Boom Boom Boom). Rub with Garlic.
Saute Green peppers, mushrooms, oregano and
Garlic in oil. Remove. Add meat to oil. Brown.
Add tomatoes and Beef Bouillon. Cover and
Cook 15 min. Add Sherry, soy sauce, water,
cornstarch, salt and sugar mixture.

Serve over Rice, Noodles or whatever.

This is one tasty dish.

MEAT-PIE ROMA

1½ LB. GROUND BEEF
½ C. CHOPPED GREEN PEPPER
1 jar spaGHetti sauce
1 8oz. tin (Biscuits) Biscuits
1 C. parmesan CHeese
1 can musHROoms
1 12 oz. MozzaRella CHeese (SHRedded)
1 sm. CHopped onion

Place Biscuits in pie tin and press to form cRust. BROwn meat and dRain off fat. Add onion, GReen peppeR, MUSHROoms and sauce. SpRinkle with parmesan CHeese. Scoop into pie tin. AlteRnate meat and MozzaRella in layeRs.
   Bake at 400° foR 15-20 min.

MAMMA MIA!
VIVA LA CUCINA!
(tR: lonG live tHe Kitchen)

65.

·〰〰· CHICKEN ParMesan ·〰〰·

1 package Onion Soup Mix
1 can Mushroom Soup
1 soup can of Milk
1 soup can of white wine
1 ¼ c. uncooked Rice
6-8 pieces Chicken
Salt and Pepper
¼ - ½ stick of Butter (or margarine)
Grated Parmesan Cheese

Preheat oven to 325°. Mix first 5 ingredients together in 9" x 13" pan or casserole.
Place chicken on top of mixture.
Sprinkle with salt and pepper.
Put thin slice → □ of butter on each piece of chicken. Bake 1 hour.
Sprinkle with cheese.
Bake 15 minutes more.

★ Beef Burgundy ★

2 tbls. shortening
5 med. onions, sliced
½ LB. Mushrooms, sliced
2 LBs. Round steak cut
    into 1" cubes
¾ c. Beef Bouillon
1½ c. Red Burgundy

1 tsp. salt
¼ tsp. Marjoram
    leaves
¼ tsp. thyme
⅛ tsp. pepper
1½ tbls. flour

In melted shortening, cook onions and mushrooms until tender. Remove.
In same skillet, brown meat; add more shortening if necessary. Sprinkle seasonings and herbs over meat. Mix flour and bouillon; stir into skillet. Heat to boiling, stirring constantly. Boil and stir 1 minute. Stir in wine. Cover and simmer 1½-2 hrs. or until meat is tender. (Liquid should always just cover meat. If necessary add more bouillon and wine — 1 part bouillon to 2 parts wine.)
    Gently stir in onions and mushrooms; cook 15 min. or until heated through.
4-6 servings.

The Sunbeam Poem

She was a sunbeam all sparkling
   and bright,
Shedding her rays from left and
   from right.
She was a sunbeam with zeal
   unabated,
She was a sunbeam and boy
   was she hated.

Valentina
Wisiniewski

*SLOPPY JOSEPHINES

2 LBS. GROUND CHUCK
1 onion CHOPPED
BROWN BOTH in skillet.
THEN add:
2 stalks CHOPPED CELERY
1 C. Catsup
SPLASH of SHERRY
¼ c. WATER
1 tsp. SALT
PEPPER
GREEN pepper if you want.

COOK. SimmER... aBOUT 20 min.
SERVE on HAMBURGER
BUNS.

* contRiButes to THE feminist
CHARACTER of THiS COOKBOOK.

BEEF AND BEER

2 tsp. M.S.G.
1/4 c. flour
1 1/2 tsp. salt
1/4 tsp. pepper
1 Bay Leaf
1/4 tsp. thyme

1/4 c. Butter
4 med. onions - sliced
12 oz. Beer
2 Tbsp. parsley flakes
2 lbs. Boneless Beef cut
   to 1" cubes

Mix M.S.G, flour, salt and pepper.
Roll pieces of Beef in mix. Heat
Butter in dutch oven. Add onions
and cook till tender. Remove onions.
Add Beef and Brown on all sides.
Return onions. Add Beer and other
ingredients. Cover. Cook on low heat
for 2 hours.

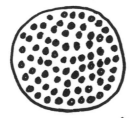

THERE are 336 dimples on a
REGULATION GOLFBALL.

BROCCOLI CASSEROLE

¼ c. chopped onion
4 tbsp. margarine
2 tbsp. flour
½ c. water
1 8oz. Cheez-Whiz
2 pk. 10 oz. frozen broccoli
3 eggs
½ c. crushed crackers

Saute onions in 4 tbsp. margarine until soft. Stir in flour, add water, cook over low heat till it boils, blend in cheese; combine sauce and broccoli, add eggs and crumbs. Mix gently. Put in 1½ qt. casserole. Bake 350° for 30 min.
This will really grab you.

Skillet Lasagna

10 Lasagna noodles, cooked
1 LB. Ground Beef
1 sm. onion minced
1 sm. jar Spaghetti sauce
15 oz. Ricotta cheese
1 egg
1/4 tsp. salt
1/4 tsp. pepper
8 oz. Shredded Mozzarella

In a 12oz. skillet cook Beef and onion about 10 min. Stir in 2/3 sauce Cook until Heated through. Spoon 1/2 of meat mixture into small Bowl... set aside. In medium Bowl combine Ricotta, egg, salt and pepper. Spoon 1/2 of Ricotta on meat mixture in skillet. Top with 1/2 Lasagna noodles. Sprinkle with 1/2 Mozzarella. Repeat Layering with meat, Ricotta, Lasagna noodles, sauce and Mozzarella Cover. Cook 5min. till Heated through.

~ A LITTLE KNOWN FACT ~

Baby Face Nelson's Real name is Lester Gillis (not Michael dongarra).

72.

MAGNIFICENT MEAT
★ ★ ★ LOAF ★ ★ ★

CRUMBLE 2 cups of stale BREAD. THen Mince ¾ c. onion and ¼ c. GReen pepper. Heat oven to 400°. THen BReak 2 eGGs into a LaRGe BOWL. AfteR Beating them sLiGHtLy add the GRound meat (2 LBS.). LiGHtLy Mix the eGGs and meat toGetHeR. Next add the BRead cRumBs, onion and GReen pepper. THen add 2 tBsp. HORSe RadisH, 1 tBsp. salt, 1 tsp. dry mustard, ¼ c. MiLk and ¼ c. catsup. THen aGain mix LiGHtLy But well. Now sHape meat into a Loaf→ [□]. GRease a sHaLLow Baking disH. Put the Loaf in. Spread ½ c. catsup oveR Loaf, then Bake foR 40 min.

Remember
You can't Have youR BRead
and Loaf too.

73.

SALAD SUPERB

(even dearly loved by people
who hate salads)

In a big salad bowl place in order:
1 head torn lettuce
3 lrg. stalks chopped celery
1 onion sliced in rings ⊚⊚⊚⊚⊚⊚
1 cucumber chopped up

Then mix 1 c. sour cream and
½ c. sugar and pour over orderly
layered salad.

Then mix 4 Tbsp. vinegar and
½ c. salad dressing or mayonnaise...
and pour over first salad dressing.

Then sprinkle 1 lb. crumbled bacon fried
crisp over the top of the salad and
top off with a few shakes of
parmesan cheese, maybe some
croutons, egg slices, whatever.

Fix at least 2-4 hrs. ahead.

(FIVE STAR SOUR CREAM CHICKEN)

8 CHICKEN BREASTS BOILED (FOR
   1-1½ HRS.)
SALT and PEPPER CHICKEN. z·z· z·z· z· z·z·z
Let CHICKEN SLEEP in JUICES
   overNIGHt.
Bone CHICKEN and CUt into
   LITTLE CUBES ◻◻◻◻◻◻ .

SAUCE: 1 PINT SOUR CREAM
         2 CANS MUSHROOM SOUP
MIX. MaKe a sauce, add tHe CHICKEN,
some canned OR fresH MUSHROOMS
and a few SHaKeS of GaRLIC
SaLt· If it's too tHICK add some
MILK.
      BaKe at 300° foR 2 HRS.
   SeRve over RICE OR noodLes.

MEMERÉ'S TOUQUÉ PIE
(GRANDMOTHER'S PORK PIE)

2 LBS. GROUND PORK
¼ LB. GROUND CHUCK
1 LRG. onion finely chopped

COOK MEAT. DRAIN off fat and add a little water. Add salt, pepper, POULTRY dressing and sage to taste.

COOK two or three medium potatoes. MASH. Add to meat mixture.

PREPARE PIE CRUST:

Sift 2 c. flour -- dash or two of salt -- mix with ⅔ c. SHORTENING. That makes crust dough. ROLL OUT for top and bottom crust.

Place cooked meat in crust. Cover with top crust. Slit top. BRUSH top crust with MILK. Bake at 400° until crust is brown. Serve with catsup if you like it that way.

POLISH PIGS IN A BLANKET

2 LBS. GROUND BEEF
¼ C. COOKED RICE
1 CHOPPED ONION FRIED BROWN
1 HEAD CABBAGE
1 CAN TOMATO SOUP.
1 SOUP CAN WATER
BACON

Mix Beef and Rice, salt and pepper to taste, add onion. Cook cabbage for ½ HR. Fill cooked cabbage leaves with meat mixture, ROLL. Then put in a BIG Baking dish, cover with tomato soup and put a few strips of Bacon on top. Bake for 1½ HRS. at 350°.

WAIT UNTIL YOU HEAR THIS.

The United States department of Agriculture advises that the best time to spray Household insects is at 4:00 p.m. This is their High Vulnerability time.

77.

GOOD 'OL CREOLE
~ ROUNDSTEAK ~

1 c. Bread crumbs
½ c. minced celery
¾ c. minced onion
¼ c. melted butter
1 tbsp. chopped parsley
1½ tsp. salt
⅛ tsp. pepper
1 tsp. sage
2 c. canned tomatoes
½ c. green peppers
3 tbsp. shortening
1½ lbs. Round O steak
8 or 10 small potatoes

Combine the first eight ingredients. Saute steak in shortening until lightly browned. Spread mixture on steak, roll and tie → 🌀. Put in casserole; add tomatoes and green pepper. Cover and bake 2 hrs. (not 🎀 but 🎀) at 350°. Add potatoes last 45 min.

(CHILLY? CHILI.)

1½ LB. Ground Beef
1 c. chopped onion
1 c. chopped green pepper
1 c. tomatoes
18 oz. tomato sauce
3 tsp. chili powder
2 tsp. salt
¼ tsp. pepper
⅛ tsp. paprika
1 can kidney beans
2 dashes hot sauce
1 c. chopped celery (optional)

Fry meat, onion and green pepper till meat gets brown. Stir in everything else. Heat to boiling... Reduce heat. Cover and simmer two hours.

Serve with crackers and cheddar cheese chunks.
"Cheese," is this good!

★ P. C. T. ★

(POPOVER CHICKEN TARRAGON)

Brown 2 LBS. Chicken parts in oil. Season with salt and pepper.

In a separate Bowl →  Blend 3 eggs, 1½ c. milk and 1 Tbsp. vegetable oil.

Stir together 1½ c. flour, ¾ tsp. salt and 1 tsp. tarragon. Add to egg mixture and Beat till smooth.

Pour over chicken. Bake in 9"x13" dish - uncovered - at 350° for 55-60 min.

If you're wild about tarragon you can sprinkle some more on before you pop it in the oven.

Beer Batter for Fish

1 c. flour
1 tbsp. paprika
1 tsp. salt
1 egg
1 12 oz. can beer
Lemon juice (preferably fresh)
oil

Sift together flour, paprika and salt. Then gradually beat in egg and beer until the batter is quite thin. While the fish is waiting on the platter squeeze some lemon over it. On a separate plate put flour to dip fish in. Then take the fish, dip it in the batter, then dip it in the flour (both sides). Fry in oil for about 5-6 min.

Even if you hate fish you might love this. Terrific with lake perch.

81.

BREAD STUFFING

about 8 slices of white bread
3/4 lb. ground sausage meat
1/2 stick of butter
1/2 c. chopped celery
3/4 c. chopped onion
1/4 c. chopped parsley
1/2 tsp. poultry seasoning (preferably Bell's)
1/2 tsp. sage
1/2 c. chicken bouillon
1 egg
salt and pepper

First toast the bread lightly and cut into itty bitty cubes. Put in a bowl. Then put the sausage in a pan and cook lightly. Drain off fat. Put sausage in with itty bitty bread cubes and mix. Then mix celery and onion in the pan, cook lightly until onions smell good. (Mix with a wooden spoon.) Add that to bread mixture. Beat the egg lightly. Mix in. Add parsley and seasonings. Mix. Add bouillon (or stock) a little at a time, mixing well. Salt and pepper to taste. Stuff in turkey (enough for a 10 lb. biggie) or put in casserole dish and bake at 350° for 1 1/2 hrs. or so.

Jello Extraordinaire

2 pks. strawberry jello
1 can crushed pineapple (10 oz.)
1 lrg. container frozen strawberries
2 c. boiling water
1 pt. sour cream
2 mashed bananas

Dissolve jello in water. Let cool. Add pineapple, bananas and strawberries. Put ½ of mixture in pan... Refrigerate till it sets. Keep other half of mixture at room temperature. After first half sets spread layer of sour cream, then add rest of jello mixture. Refrigerate until it's all set.

THIS IS SO GOOD.

TOMATO CHEESE STRATA

1 loaf French Bread cut into 1" slices
3/4 stick of butter
1/2 c. chopped onion
1 chopped Green pepper
2 tsp. sugar

1 crushed garlic clove
1 tsp. oregano
1 tsp. pepper
8 tomatoes (sliced)
1 LB. mozzarella sliced
2 tsp. salt

Bake bread at 400° till brown. Then cut into cubes. In a frying pan heat butter, onion, green pepper, garlic, sugar, oregano, salt and pepper. Simmer about 8-10 min. Then grease 9x13 baking pan. Put bread cubes in. Spread 1/2 of mixture over bread cubes. Then take tomato slices and fix them in overlapping rows of tomatoes and cheese on top of the mixture. Spoon rest of mixture on top of that, cover with foil and bake at 400° for 10 min. Uncover and bake about 5 min. more. You'll dream about this one.

PIZZA CASSEROLE

1½ LB. BULK pizza sausage
2 TBSP. oil
1 onion chopped
1 tsp. salt
½ tsp. pepper
2 cans pizza sauce (12oz.)
¼ tsp. oregano
½ tsp. Italian seasoning
¼ tsp. garlic salt
1 c. milk
1 egg
1 7oz. pkg. elbow macaroni, cooked
1 c. shredded mozzarella cheese

Brown meat and onion in oil; add pizza sauce and seasonings. Drain cooked macaroni. Beat egg and milk and add macaroni. Spread macaroni mixture in 9x13 pan. Cover with meat mixture. Bake at 350° for 15 min. Remove and sprinkle cheese over casserole and return to oven for 15 min. more. Let stand and cool its jets 10 min. then cut. (If bulk pizza sausage is unavailable, use Italian sausage, removed from the casing and eliminate the spices.)

★ ZUCCHINI ZINGER ★

3 c. thinly sliced unpeeled zucchini

1/2 c. uncooked Rice

1/2 c. onion chopped

1/4 c. parsley

1 chopped Garlic clove

1 1/2 tsp. salt

3 eggs Beaten

3/4 c. Milk

1 c. shredded sharp cheese

1/2 tsp. pepper

3/4 c. Boiling water

Heat oven to 350°. In a LARGE sauce pan mix zucchini, Rice, onion, parsley, Garlic, salt and pepper. Add Boiling water, Cover and cook 15 min. on Low Heat then remove. Mix eggs, Milk and cheese. Pour and stir into zucchini and Rice mixture. Pour that into 1 1/2 qt. casserole dish. Cover and Bake 25 min. Uncover and Bake 5 min. more. Sprinkling Bread crumbs on top Before Baking Gives it Real pizzazz.

SPICES: the variety in Life

Spices and when to use them

Allspice: pot Roasts, squash, fish, eggs, even sweet potatoes.

Basil: an indispensable spice: tomatoes, noodles, pork, Meat loaf, noodles, fish, veal, eggplant, carrots, potatoes, stews and Rice.

Bay Leaf: soups, chowders, pot Roasts, stews, tomato sauces, marinades.

Cayenne pepper: spaghetti, pizza, chicken, fish, veggies, Meat dishes.

Garlic: tomato dishes, soups, dips, sauces, put it in everything and chew a lot of gum.

Onion Powder: soups, stews, Meats, chicken, fish, salads, veggies, almost anything.

Oregano: All things italian, chili, BBQ sauce, veggie soup, stuffing, omelets, chicken.

Poultry Seasoning: stuffings, chicken, turkey. Meat loaf, meat pies.

Paprika: Beef, pork, veal, sausage, fish, chicken, veggies one and all, anything that needs color.

*__Parsley__: Soups, coleslaw, tomato sauces, stuffings, fish, decoration.

*__Sage__: stuffings, fish, meats, sauces, soups, chowders, marinades, tomatoes, chicken, fish, pork, almost anything.

*__Rosemary__: poultry, veal, beef, pork, stews, fish, marinades, tatoes, cauliflower and spinach.

*__Thyme__: meat, poultry, fish, veggies.

__Fennel seed__: egg dishes, fish, stews, meat marinades, veggies.

__Sherry__: splash it in everything.

*wouldn't that make a good song?

SLEEP

God speaks:

I don't like the man who doesn't sleep, says God.

I am talking about those who work and don't sleep.

I pity them. I have it against them. A little. They won't trust me.

They have the courage to work.
They lack the courage to be idle.

To stretch out. To rest. To sleep.
Poor people, they don't know what is good.
He who doesn't sleep is unfaithful to hope.
They look after their business very well
  during the day.
But they haven't enough confidence in me
  to let me look after it during the night.
As if I wasn't capable of looking after
  it during one night.
Human wisdom says, Don't put off until
  tomorrow what can be done the very
  same day.

90.

And I tell you: Put off until tomorrow
 those worries and those troubles which
 are gnawing at you today...
And might very well devour you today.
 Put off until tomorrow those tears which
fill your eyes and your head,
 Flooding you, rolling down your cheeks,
 those tears which stream down your
   cheeks.
Because between now and tomorrow, maybe
 I, God, will have passed your way.
Human wisdom says: Woe to the man who
 puts off what he has to do until tomorrow.
And I say Blessed, Blessed is the man who
 puts off what he has to do until
 tomorrow.
Blessed is he who puts off. That is to say
 Blessed is he who hopes. And who sleeps.

                    — Charles Péguy